Animal
JOKES

By **U.R. Phunny**

BIG BUDDY

JOKES

Big Buddy Books
An imprint of Abdo Publishing
abdopublishing.com

abdopublishing.com

Published by Abdo Publishing, a division of ABDO, PO Box 398166, Minneapolis, Minnesota 55439. Copyright © 2017 by Abdo Consulting Group, Inc. International copyrights reserved in all countries. No part of this book may be reproduced in any form without written permission from the publisher. Big Buddy Books™ is a trademark and logo of Abdo Publishing.

Printed in the United States of America, North Mankato, Minnesota.
082016
012017

Illustrations: Sunny Grey/Spectrum Studio

Coordinating Series Editor: Tamara L. Britton
Contributing Editor: Katie Lajiness
Graphic Design: Taylor Higgins

Publisher's Cataloging-in-Publication Data

Names: Phunny, U. R., author.
Title: Animal jokes / by U. R. Phunny.
Description: Minneapolis, MN : Abdo Publishing, 2017. | Series: Big buddy jokes
Identifiers: LCCN 2016944866 | ISBN 9781680785104 (lib. bdg.) | ISBN
    9781680798708 (ebook)
Subjects: LCSH: Animals--Juvenile humor. | Wit and humor--Juvenile humor.
Classification: DDC 818/.602--dc23
LC record available at http://lccn.loc.gov/2016944866

What part of a fish weighs the most?

Its scales!

3

What sound do porcupines make when they kiss?

Ouch!

What did the duck say when he'd finished shopping?

Put it on my bill please.

What do ducks watch on TV?

Duck-umentaries!

Why did the dolphin cross the beach?

To get to the other tide.

5

What is the easiest way to count a herd of cows?

Use a cow-culator.

What do you call a sleeping bull?

A bulldozer.

What's the difference between a cat and a frog?

A cat has nine lives, but a frog croaks every night!

What do you call a crate of ducks?

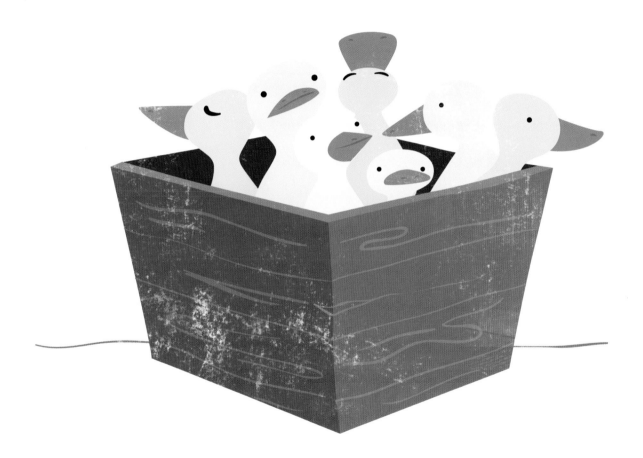

A box of quackers!

Why did the foal go to the doctor?

Because he was a little horse!

Why are elephants never rich?

Because they work for peanuts.

What do you get when you cross a frog and a rabbit?

A rabbit that says "ribbit."

Why did the lamb run over the cliff?

He didn't see the ewe turn!

Why did the rooster cross the road?

To cock-a-doodle-doo something.

Why did the chicken cross the road, roll in the mud, and cross the road again?

Because she was a dirty double-crosser.

Why did the dog go to court?

Because he got a barking ticket.

Did you hear the story about the skunk?

Never mind, it stinks.

What kind of ties do pigs wear?

Pig sties!

What bird can be heard at mealtimes?

A swallow.

What's a funny fish called?

A clownfish!

Why do cows like jokes?

Because they like to be a-moosed!

13

What kind of ant is even bigger than an elephant?

A gi-ant!

What do you say if you meet a toad?

Wart's new?

How does a pig go to the hospital?

In a ham-bulance.

What's in the middle of a jellyfish?

Its jelly-button.

What do you call a chicken at the North Pole?

Lost.

What do you call a gorilla wearing earmuffs?

Anything you like, he can't hear you.

Why do fish swim in salt water?

Because pepper makes them sneeze!

Why do birds fly south in the winter?

Because it's too far to walk!

What do you call an arctic cow?

An eski-moo!

What do you call a frog who wants to be a cowboy?

Hopalong Cassidy!

What would you see at a chicken show?

Hen-tertainment.

Why did the turkey cross the road?

To prove she wasn't chicken.

What's big and gray and wears glass slippers?

Cinderella-phant.

What do you get when you cross a cow with a duck?

Cheese and quackers.

What did the pig do when the pen broke?

Used a pig pencil.

What do you get if you cross a teddy bear with a pig?

A teddy boar!

What is worse than an alligator with a toothache?

A centipede with athlete's foot!

What game do cows play at parties?

Moo-sical chairs.

What do whales eat?

Fish and ships.

Why are giraffes so slow to apologize?

It takes them a long time to swallow their pride.

What's the difference between a fish and a piano?

You can't tuna fish.

Why should you avoid playing cards in the jungle?

Because there are so many cheetahs.

Where did the lamb get a haircut?

The Baaaaa Baaaaa Shop.

What happened when the chicken slept under the car?

She woke up oily the next morning.

What do you get if you cross a shark with a parrot?

A creature that talks your head off.

What animal would you like to be on a cold day?

A little otter!

How do you catch a squirrel?

Climb up a tree and act like a nut!

Why can't you play jokes on snakes?

Because you can never pull their legs.

27

What did the banana do when the monkey chased it?

The banana split.

What do you call a cow lying on the floor?

Ground beef.

What did the mother bee say to the baby bee?

Behive yourself!

What do cows do on a Saturday night?

They go to the moooo-vies!

What did the buffalo say to his son when he left for college?

Bison!

What do you call a horse that lives next door?

A neigh-bor.

What do you call a girl cow in Spanish?

Moo-chacha.

30

What did the snail say when it went for a ride on the turtle's back?

Whee!

WEBSITES

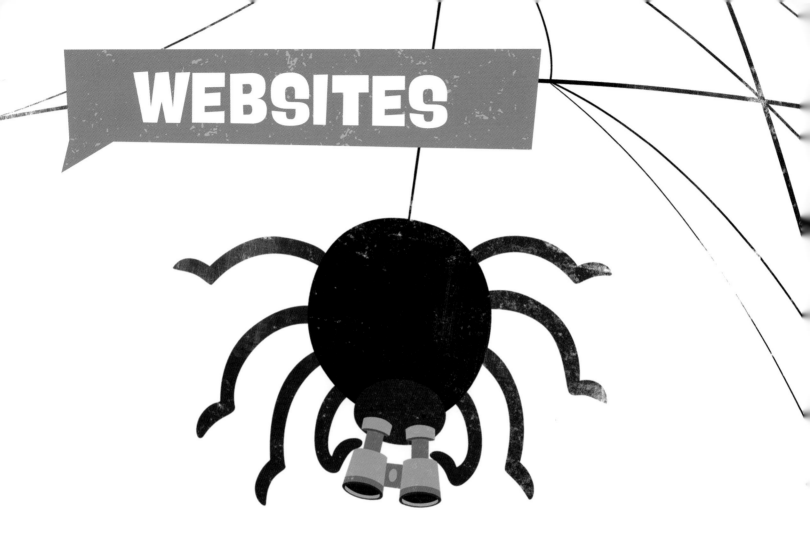